salsas & dips

salsas & dips

hamlyn

NOTES

The Department of Health advises that eggs should not be consumed raw. This book contains some dishes made with raw or lightly cooked eggs. It is prudent for more vulnerable people such as pregnant and nursing mothers, invalids, the elderly, babies and young children to avoid uncooked or lightly cooked dishes made with eggs.

Meat and poultry should be cooked thoroughly. To test if poultry is cooked, pierce the flesh through the thickest part with a skewer or fork – the juices should run clear, never pink or red. Keep refrigerated until ready for cooking.

This book includes dishes made with nuts and nut derivatives. It is advisable for those with known allergic reactions to nuts and nut derivatives and those who may be potentially vulnerable to these allergies, such as pregnant and nursing mothers, invalids, the elderly, babies and children, to avoid dishes made with nuts and nut oils. It is also prudent to check the labels of preprepared ingredients for the possible inclusion of nut derivatives.

First published in Great Britain in 2003 by
Hamlyn, a division of Octopus Publishing Group Ltd
2–4 Heron Quays, London E14 4JP

ISBN 0 600 60780 1

A CIP catalogue record for this book is available from the British Library

Printed and bound in China

10 9 8 7 6 5 4 3 2 1

contents

introduction

Salsas and dips are popularly served with tortilla chips, potato chips or vegetable sticks and served as finger food at parties, as 'nibbles' with pre-dinner drinks or as a meal appetizer. However, the versatility of salsas and dips means their use extends way beyond 'chips 'n' dips'. A spoonful or two of either is just as likely to be served in a bun with a burger, as a topping for crostini, as a filling for baked potatoes, or as an accompaniment to salad or grilled, roasted or barbecued meat, poultry and fish.

Salsas

The word 'salsa' means 'sauce' in Spanish, but is now widely used to describe a type of relish comprising a colourful mixture of finely diced vegetables and/or fruit and seasonings – in effect a crunchy 'salad'. Salsas are usually made with uncooked ingredients, less common are salsas that are cooked and puréed. Mexican in origin and often spicy, salsas can range from mild to fiery hot. Nowadays, salsas are popular almost everywhere and the scope for suitable salsa ingredients has widened dramatically from the ripe tomatoes – or tomatillos for green salsa (*salsa verde*) – onion, garlic, chillies and fresh coriander of a traditional Mexican salsa.

Virtually anything goes, so be inspired by the recipes on pages 10–27 and feel free to experiment. Try combining different fruits and vegetables with onions and/or garlic and chillies and/or peppers, together with sweet (fruit juice, honey or sugar) and sour (lime juice, lemon juice or a vinegar) flavours plus salt and black pepper. Optional extras could include olive oil, finely grated fresh root ginger, chopped olives, mustard seeds and chopped fresh herbs such as coriander, mint, sage or parsley.

Uses for salsa

Although salsas are available bottled, or fresh from the delicatessen counter, you cannot beat the taste of a homemade salsa. Aside from their popular partnership with tortilla chips and taco shells, salsas are ideal for adding depth and flavour to a meal.

Being colourful, salsas make effective garnishes, while their raw crunchiness adds texture to soup or a toasted cheese sandwich. As a relish on the side, mild salsas are refreshing with a hot curry, while spicier versions make a tasty accompaniment to plainly cooked meats and fish like steamed salmon or chicken. Just as traditional fruit sauces are served with roasted pork, ham and duck to cut their richness, fruity salsas with their zingy citrus/vinegar content can perform the same function. Tomato-based salsas make good bases for pizza toppings and pasta sauces and work well with scrambled or poached eggs. A fruity salsa made without onions makes a refreshing dessert.

Making salsa:

Salsas are simple to make and require just a sharp knife for fine dicing. Alternatively, you can use a food processor, but do make use of its pulse button so that the ingredients retain some texture instead of being pulverized. You can even buy a manually operated, purpose-made salsa maker, whose hand-cranked blade chops salsa ingredients to perfection.

The fruits and vegetables in salsas are usually used fresh although sun-dried or canned tomatoes, dried chillies, canned sweetcorn and canned pineapple can all be used in a salsa. In addition, some ingredients benefit from light cooking before use to intensify their flavour – roasted peppers and chargrilled sweetcorn are good examples.

Dips

Whereas the origins of salsa lie in Mexican and southwestern American cooking, dips originate from all over the globe, as the recipes on pages 28–47 demonstrate. From Mexico to Europe, the Middle East and Far East, every cuisine has its favourite dip and 'dipper' – think of guacamole and tortilla chips, aïoli and French bread, hummus or baba ganoush and pitta bread, raita and poppadums, peanut sauce and chicken skewers.

Dips make entertaining easy – most can be made in advance – and they are always popular with guests. Simply present people with a choice of dips, dippers and a napkin and let them help themselves. Use any leftover dip in sandwiches or baked potatoes, or as the basis for a sauce for pasta, rice or noodles.

Shortcut dippers

There are plenty of suggestions for homemade accompaniments for dips
on pages 48–63 – from straightforward potato wedges to the more involved
vegetable tempura and beef satays for a special occasion. If time is short,
however, shop-bought standbys include bread sticks (available in mini
lengths), tortillas, potato chips (scoop-shaped or ridged ones are perfect
for dipping), corn chips, cheese straws, vegetable chips, rice cakes,
pretzels, mini pitta breads or any of the appealing speciality breads now
widely available.

Vegetable crudités are another quick option. Many supermarkets offer
a selection of baby vegetables, such as baby corn and baby carrots, which
are just the right size for dipping. Sugar snap peas, cherry tomatoes and
button mushrooms are also ideal sizes while vegetables such as celery,
peppers, cucumber and courgettes require cutting to length and cauliflower
and broccoli need breaking into florets. Again, to save time, many of these
can be bought ready prepared.

Watching your weight?

Happily, salsas are low in fat and low in calories, if you need to be vigilant
about what you eat. They are also packed with vitamins and are rich in fibre
so are a healthy option. You need to be a little more careful when choosing
a dip – and of course what you use to dip into it! Many dips are based on
cream, mayonnaise or cream cheese. Some recipes can be adapted to use
low-fat ingredients like fromage frais and plain yogurt – raita is a good
example – but can suffer from a loss of flavour as a result. However, low-fat
mayonnaise, half-fat cream cheese and half-fat crème fraîche can often be
substituted for the real thing and are a good compromise with regard to
flavour and fat content. Vegetable crudités, pitta bread, pretzels and
breadsticks are healthier accompaniments than crisps and cheesy crackers.

1 **red onion**, finely chopped

425 g (14 oz) small
vine-ripened tomatoes,
halved, deseeded and
chopped

2 **garlic cloves**, crushed

15 g ($^{1}/_{2}$ oz) **coriander
leaves**, chopped

salt and **pepper**

coriander and tomato salsa

1 Put the red onion, tomatoes, garlic and coriander leaves in a bowl and mix together. Season lightly with salt and pepper, then cover and chill for at least 30 minutes for the flavours to develop.

2 Serve with cold meats or as a side dish with curries and other spicy foods.

Makes 350 ml (12 fl oz)

Preparation time: 10 minutes, plus chilling

2–3 tablespoons **lime juice**

1 tablespoon **olive oil**

a few drops of **Tabasco sauce**

1 small **garlic clove**, finely chopped

$^1/_2$ small **red onion**, finely chopped

2 large firm, ripe **tomatoes**, skinned, deseeded and finely chopped

2 large firm, ripe **avocados**, halved, stoned, peeled and chopped

2 tablespoons finely chopped **coriander leaves**

salt and **pepper**

avocado and tomato salsa

1 Put the lime juice, olive oil, Tabasco and garlic in a bowl and whisk well to combine. Stir in the onion, add the chopped tomato and avocado and toss gently in the dressing along with the chopped coriander. Season to taste with salt and pepper.

Makes 400 ml (14 fl oz)

Preparation time: 10 minutes

TIP

A ripe avocado gives slightly when you press it at the pointed end. However, if you have an unripe avocado and need to speed up the ripening process, put it in a paper bag with an apple or a banana. The gases they give off help to accelerate ripening.

black bean, tomato and coriander salsa

1 Drain the black beans and cook in a saucepan of salted boiling water for 45 minutes or according to the packet instructions. Cool under cold running water and drain thoroughly.

2 Put the black beans into a bowl and add the chopped tomatoes, red and green chillies, garlic, lime rind and juice, olive oil and coriander leaves. Season generously with salt and pepper, then cover and leave to stand for 30 minutes before serving for the flavours to infuse.

Makes 400 ml (14 fl oz)

Preparation time: 15 minutes, plus standing

Cooking time: 45 minutes

FOOD FACT
The black bean is also known as the turtle, Mexican or Spanish black bean and black kidney bean. It is widely used in Latin American cooking and in recipes from the Southwest of the USA. It has a white inside and mild flavour and should not be confused with the Asian or Chinese black bean, a type of soya bean which is salted and used as a flavouring.

75 g (3 oz) **black beans**, soaked for 8 hours or overnight

5 **plum tomatoes**, skinned and chopped

1 large **red chilli**, deseeded and finely chopped

1 large **green chilli**, deseeded and finely chopped

2 **garlic cloves**, finely chopped

grated rind and juice of 1 **lime**

2 tablespoons **olive oil**

3 tablespoons chopped **coriander leaves**

salt and **pepper**

5 **tomatillos**

2 **jalapeño chillies**, deseeded and finely chopped

2 **garlic cloves**, finely chopped

$^1/_2$ **red onion**, finely chopped

2 tablespoons chopped **basil**

1 tablespoon **clear honey**

1 tablespoon **olive oil**

salt and **pepper**

green tomatillo salsa

Despite their name, tomatillos, which come from Mexico, belong to the same family as physalis and Chinese lanterns and not the tomato family. If you are pushed for time you can blend all the ingredients for this salsa in a food processor; this means that the finished result may be slightly slushy, but it will still taste fantastic.

1 Remove the outer leaves from the tomatillos and wash them thoroughly to remove any stickiness from the skins. Chop them finely and put them into a bowl with the chillies, garlic, onion, basil, honey and olive oil. Mix well and season generously with salt and pepper. Serve immediately.

Makes 400 ml (14 fl oz)

Preparation time: 15 minutes

1 small **red onion**, finely chopped

1 **garlic clove**, finely chopped

500 g (1 lb) sweet ripe **tomatoes**, skinned, deseeded and chopped

1–2 sweet, moderately hot **red chillies**, deseeded and finely chopped

3 tablespoons finely chopped **coriander leaves**

1 tablespoon finely chopped **parsley**

1 tablespoon **lime juice**

3 tablespoons **olive oil**

pinch of **sugar**

salt and **pepper**

hot tomato salsa

This is a very useful basic tomato salsa. For variety, you can add chopped fresh herbs, such as mint, fennel, lovage, oregano, marjoram, dill and tarragon. For a more gentle salsa, leave out the chilli.

1 Put the onion, garlic, tomatoes and chillies into a bowl. Add the coriander and parsley and stir in the lime juice and olive oil. Season with a pinch of sugar and salt and pepper and mix lightly.

2 Cover and chill for 30–60 minutes, to let the flavours develop before serving.

Makes 375 ml (13 fl oz)

Preparation time: 10–15 minutes, plus chilling

cucumber salsa

1 Halve the cucumber lengthways and scoop out the seeds. Finely chop the cucumber and toss in a bowl with the coriander, spring onions, lemon or lime juice, sugar and a little salt and pepper. Cover and chill for at least 30 minutes for the flavours to develop.

2 Serve with cold meats or burgers and a mixed salad.

Makes 300 ml ($^{1}/_{2}$ pint)

Preparation time: 10 minutes, plus chilling

$^{1}/_{2}$ small **cucumber**

2 tablespoons chopped **coriander leaves**

2 **spring onions**, finely chopped

1 tablespoon **lemon** or **lime juice**

1 teaspoon **caster sugar**

salt and **pepper**

2 **corn cobs**, stripped of husks and threads

3 tablespoons **olive oil**

1 tablespoon **red onion**, finely chopped

3–4 tablespoons **lime juice**

2 dashes of **jalapeño sauce**

1 small **red chilli**, deseeded and finely chopped

$^1/_4$ small **red pepper**, cored, deseeded and finely chopped

1 large firm, **red plum tomato**, skinned, deseeded and finely chopped

$^1/_4$ teaspoon **ground coriander**

2 tablespoons finely chopped **coriander**

1 firm, ripe **avocado**, halved, stoned, peeled and chopped

salt and **pepper**

chargrilled sweetcorn and avocado salsa

This salsa is delicious with grilled or roasted meats and fish. If it is kept longer than a few hours the avocado will discolour and lose its vibrancy, so make it only far enough ahead to allow the flavours to mingle and develop. Alternatively, prepare the salsa in advance without the avocado, adding it about 30 minutes before serving.

1 Plunge the corn cobs into a saucepan of boiling water, return to the boil and blanch for 3–4 minutes. Drain, rub with a little of the olive oil, and place under a preheated very hot grill for 10–15 minutes, turning occasionally, until tender and well toasted. Leave to cool slightly, then scrape the kernels into a bowl and set aside to cool.

2 Add the onion to the corn with the lime juice, jalapeño sauce, chilli, red pepper, tomato, ground and chopped coriander, the remaining oil and salt and pepper. Toss gently to combine, then fold in the avocado. Taste and adjust the seasoning as necessary. Cover and chill for at least 30 minutes for the flavours to develop.

Makes 450 ml ($^3/_4$ pint)

Preparation time: 15 minutes, plus cooling and chilling

Cooking time: 15–20 minutes

hot papaya and roasted pepper salsa

Sweet and tangy, this salsa is delicious with grilled or fried meat, chicken, fish and vegetables. It is best eaten the day it is made.

1 Combine the lime juice, olive oil and balsamic vinegar in a bowl. Add the papayas, chilli, spring onions and roasted red peppers and toss gently until combined. Season with salt and pepper and stir in the coriander. Cover and chill for about 30 minutes before serving to allow the flavours to blend and develop.

Makes 400 g (14 fl oz)

Preparation time: 10–15 minutes, plus chilling

juice of 1–2 **limes**

4 tablespoons **light olive oil**

$1/4$ teaspoon **balsamic vinegar**

2 ripe **papayas**, peeled, deseeded and cut into 1 cm ($1/2$ inch) dice

$1/2$ small **red chilli**, finely chopped

2 **spring onions**, finely chopped

2 **roasted red peppers**, cored, deseeded and cut into 5 mm ($1/4$ inch) dice

1 tablespoon finely chopped **coriander**

salt and **pepper**

1 **papaya**, peeled, deseeded and finely chopped

juice and finely grated rind of 1 **lime**

400 g (13 oz) can **cannellini beans**, drained

2 tablespoons chopped **coriander**

2 **tomatoes**, chopped

1 small **green chilli**, deseeded and chopped

salt and **pepper**

papaya, green chilli and cannellini bean salsa

1 Mix the chopped papaya with the lime juice and the grated lime rind. Season to taste with salt and pepper and stir in the cannellini beans, the coriander, tomatoes and the chopped green chilli. Mix well and chill until ready to serve. Serve with roast loin of pork.

Makes 400 ml (14 fl oz)

Preparation time: 10 minutes, plus chilling

mango and cucumber salsa with chilli

This salsa is quick and easy to make, and can be as fiery or as refreshing as you wish – just adjust the amount of chillies or leave them out altogether. It is excellent with roasted, fried or grilled foods, particularly herrings and salmon, but is also perfect with cold meats, such as salami, bresàola or Parma ham. It will keep for several days in the refrigerator.

1 Cut the cucumber into 2.5–5 mm ($^1/_8$–$^1/_4$ inch) dice and leave in a sieve to drain. Slice each side of the flat central stone of the mango. Discard the stone and cut each piece of mango flesh into long strips 2.5–5 mm ($^1/_8$–$^1/_4$ inch) thick. Remove the skin by slipping the knife between the flesh and skin and running it along its length. Chop into dice. Combine the cucumber and mango in a bowl.

2 Put the onion in a small bowl, cover with boiling water and soak for a few minutes. Drain and refresh under cold water, then pat dry with kitchen paper (this helps to soften the flavour of the onion).

3 Add the onion to the cucumber and mango with the rest of the ingredients. Stir gently to combine. Cover and chill for a few hours to allow the flavours to mingle and develop. Serve chilled, garnished with chopped flat leaf parsley.

Makes 600 ml (1 pint)

Preparation time: 10–15 minutes, plus chilling

$^1/_2$ **cucumber**, peeled

1 large **mango**, ripe but still firm

3 tablespoons finely chopped **red onion**

1 small **green chilli**, deseeded and finely chopped

1 tablespoon finely chopped **flat leaf parsley**

juice of $1^1/_2$ **limes**

salt and **pepper**

chopped **flat leaf parsley**, to garnish

1 tablespoon **olive oil**

2.5 cm (1 inch) piece of **fresh root ginger**, peeled and finely chopped

$^1/_2$ teaspoon **mild curry powder**

1 small **red onion**, finely chopped

1 teaspoon **black mustard seeds**

2 **peaches**, peeled, halved, stoned and cut into small cubes

juice of 1 **lemon**

2 tablespoons roughly chopped **coriander leaves**

salt and **pepper**

peach and ginger salsa

Mini poppadoms are ideal with this salsa.

1 Heat the olive oil in a frying pan. Add the ginger, curry powder, red onion and mustard seeds and cook gently for 3–4 minutes until the aromas are released.

2 Remove the pan from the heat and add the peaches and lemon juice. Season generously with salt and pepper then cover and leave to stand for 30 minutes at room temperature. Transfer the salsa to a serving bowl, stir in the coriander leaves and serve immediately.

Makes 450 ml ($^3/_4$ pint)

Preparation time: 10 minutes, plus standing

Cooking time: 3–4 minutes

150 g (5 oz) **strawberries**, hulled and roughly chopped

$1/2$ ripe **mango,** peeled, stoned and roughly chopped

$1/2$ ripe **papaya**, peeled, deseeded and roughly chopped

1 **orange**, segmented and roughly chopped

2 tablespoons **balsamic vinegar**

1 tablespoon **vodka**

2 tablespoons chopped **mint,** to decorate

summer fruit salsa

1 Put the strawberries, mango, papaya and orange into a bowl and sprinkle with the balsamic vinegar and vodka. Cover and leave to infuse for at least 30 minutes before serving, decorated with a little chopped mint.

Makes 500 ml (17 fl oz)

Preparation time: 10 minutes, plus standing

FOOD FACT

Balsamic vinegar is generally accepted to be the finest vinegar of all. A rich, sweet vinegar, it is produced in the Emilia-Romagna region of northern Italy from grape juice and aged in wooden casks for up to 50 years or more. Ancient and truly authentic balsamic vinegars have a very mellow flavour and cost huge sums of money; what is often sold as balsamic vinegar at the cheaper end of the market is not always strictly authentic but still makes a good salad dressing.

pineapple salsa with chilli, orange and mint

1 Put the slices of pineapple in a lightly oiled grill pan, sprinkle with the brown sugar, cumin and coriander and cook under a preheated grill for 5 minutes, turning once halfway through cooking. Remove from the heat and allow to cool slightly.

2 Finely chop the pineapple, place it in a bowl and mix with the sun-dried chillies, orange rind and juice, mint and vinegar. Season with salt and pepper. Cover and leave to stand for 30 minutes before serving.

Makes 450 ml (³/₄ pint)

Preparation time: 10 minutes, plus standing

Cooking time: 5 minutes

1 small **pineapple**, peeled and cut into 2.5 cm (1 inch) slices

1 tablespoon **brown sugar**

1 teaspoon ground **cumin**

1 teaspoon ground **coriander**

2 large **red sun-dried chillies**, finely chopped

grated rind and juice of 1 **orange**

3 tablespoons chopped **mint**

2 tablespoons **red wine vinegar**

salt and **pepper**

2 large ripe **avocados**, halved, stoned and peeled

juice of 1 **lime** or **lemon**

1 **garlic clove**, crushed

1 tablespoon finely chopped **onion**

1 large **tomato**, skinned, deseeded and finely chopped

1–2 fresh **green chillies**, deseeded and finely chopped

1 tablespoon finely chopped **coriander leaves**

pinch of **sugar**

salt and **pepper**

coriander sprigs, to garnish

guacamole

This thick creamy avocado purée from Mexico can be used as a dip for Crudités (see page 63), fresh Tortilla Chips (see page 52) or Pitta Chips (see page 56), or eaten Mexican-style with tortillas. It can also be used as a sauce for fish and chicken. Don't purée the avocado flesh in a food processor or blender as this produces too smooth a texture.

1 Put the avocado flesh into a bowl with the lime or lemon juice and mash with a fork to make a textured paste. Stir in the garlic, onion, tomato, chillies, coriander and sugar. Season with salt and pepper and add some extra lime or lemon juice, if required. Spoon the mixture into a serving bowl and garnish with coriander sprigs. Cover with clingfilm to help prevent discoloration and chill until required.

Makes about 500 ml (17 fl oz)

Preparation time: 10 minutes, plus chilling

25 g (1 oz) **green le Puy lentils**

1–2 tablespoons **green peppercorns in brine**, drained

2 tablespoons **Dijon mustard**

4 tablespoons **sunflower oil**

1 tablespoon **lemon juice**

1 tablespoon **warm water**

lentil, green peppercorn and mustard dip

Serve this dip with crisp robust vegetables or fried or grilled fish. It also goes well with Crudités (see page 63). It will keep in the refrigerator for several days.

1 Bring a large saucepan of water to the boil, add the lentils and return to the boil. Cook for 10–15 minutes until just tender and beginning to turn mushy. Drain and refresh under cold water until completely cold.

2 Crush the peppercorns until roughly broken using a pestle and mortar. Transfer to a bowl, stir in the mustard and gradually beat in the oil, adding a little at a time. Stir in the lemon juice, warm water and cooked lentils. Pile into a serving bowl, cover with clingfilm and chill for at least 30 minutes.

Makes 150 ml (1/4 pint)

Preparation time: 10 minutes, plus cooling and chilling

Cooking time: 10–15 minutes

baba ganoush

This Turkish spiced aubergine pâté comes in many guises, with each recipe varying slightly. Some include tahini, others yogurt; this version with its slightly unusual addition of chopped mint is particularly delicious.

1 Prick the aubergines all over with a fork and cook them in a preheated oven at 200°C (400°F), Gas Mark 6 for 20–30 minutes, until the skins wrinkle and the flesh feels collapsed, turning them halfway through cooking. Set aside to cool.

2 Squeeze the aubergines to release the moisture then slice them open and scrape the flesh into a food processor. Add the garlic, cumin, tahini, mint and tomato and process to form a fairly smooth paste then gradually blend in the oil to soften the texture. Season with salt and pepper to taste and serve with griddle bread or pitta chips.

Makes about 300 ml (^{1}/$_2$ pint)

Preparation time: 10–15 minutes

Cooking time: 20–30 minutes

2 **aubergines**

1 **garlic clove**, crushed

^{1}/$_2$ teaspoon **ground cumin**

1 tablespoon **tahini**

2 tablespoons **chopped mint**

1 **tomato**, skinned, deseeded and chopped

4–6 tablespoons **extra virgin olive oil**

salt and **pepper**

Griddle Bread (see page 57) or **Pitta Chips** (see page 56), to serve

chilli bean dip

This spicy dip is excellent with Crudités (see page 63), corn chips or Pitta Chips (see page 56). It is also good spread on bruschetta and crostini, like a pâté.

1 Halve the peppers lengthways and scrape out the seeds. Lightly brush the peppers inside and out with a little oil. Place on a lightly oiled baking sheet and roast in a preheated oven at 240°C (475°F), Gas Mark 9 for 15 minutes. Remove the peppers from the oven and leave until cool enough to handle, then peel off the skins.

2 Work the red pepper flesh, garlic and chilli in a food processor or blender until well chopped. Add the beans and paprika and continue to process until a coarse purée forms. This won't take long. Season with Tabasco, if using, and salt and pepper. With the motor running, slowly add the remaining oil to make a thick paste.

3 Pile the bean purée into a bowl and sprinkle with the chopped chives. Cover and chill until required.

Makes about 400 ml (14 fl oz)

Preparation time: 15 minutes, plus cooling and chilling

Cooking time: 15 minutes

2 large **red peppers**

2 tablespoons **olive oil**

2 **garlic cloves**, crushed

1 small **red chilli**, deseeded and finely chopped

400 g (13 oz) can **red kidney beans**, drained

$1/2$ teaspoon **paprika**

few drops of **Tabasco sauce** (optional)

salt and **pepper**

2 tablespoons snipped **chives**, to garnish

hummus

400 g (13 oz) can **chickpeas**

2 **garlic cloves**, crushed

2–3 tablespoons **lemon juice**

150 ml ($^1/_4$ pint) **tahini**

about 150 ml ($^1/_4$ pint) **olive** or **sunflower oil**

2–4 tablespoons **natural set yogurt** or **hot water**

salt and **pepper**

cayenne pepper or **paprika**, to serve

1 Drain and rinse the chickpeas then put them into a food processor or blender with the garlic, lemon juice, tahini and salt and pepper to taste. Process to a smooth paste.

2 Very gradually add the oil as if making mayonnaise (see below). Stir in the yogurt or hot water to give the required consistency. Adjust the seasoning to taste.

3 Spoon the hummus into a serving dish and smooth with the back of a spoon. Pour over a little oil and dust with a sprinkling of cayenne or paprika.

Makes 300–350 ml (10–12 fl oz)

Preparation time: 10 minutes

aïoli, allioli or garlic mayonnaise

2–8 **garlic cloves**, according to taste

$^1/_2$ teaspoon **sea salt**

2 **egg yolks**

1 tablespoon **lemon juice**

1 teaspoon **Dijon mustard**

300 ml ($^1/_2$ pint) French **extra virgin olive oil**

1–2 teaspoons **boiling water** (optional)

1 Crush the garlic cloves with the sea salt in a mortar or by pounding them together on a board with the side of a knife blade. Transfer to a food processor with the egg yolks, lemon juice and mustard and process briefly until pale.

2 With the motor running, add the oil in a steady stream through the feeder funnel until the sauce is emulsified, thick and glossy. You may need to thin it slightly by whisking in a spoonful or two of boiling water. Cover the surface with clingfilm and chill until required.

Makes about 300 ml ($^1/_2$ pint)

Preparation time: 10 minutes, plus chilling

tapenade

The word tapenade comes from 'tapeno', the old Provençal word for caper, traditionally an important ingredient. Nowadays capers are used less frequently and sometimes they are left out altogether. Tapenade will keep in a tightly covered jar in the refrigerator for several weeks.

1 Pound the olives, capers, anchovies, garlic and mustard in a mortar to make a paste. Transfer them to a bowl and work in the oil a drop at a time initially, then add it a little more quickly. Mix in the thyme, lemon juice and plenty of black pepper. Adjust the consistency (it should be a thick, spreadable paste) and pungency if necessary, adding more oil to mellow it. Serve at room temperature.

Makes 375 ml (13 fl oz)

Preparation time: 10 minutes

200 g (7 oz) Noyons **black olives**, pitted

50 g (2 oz) **capers**

4 **anchovy fillets**, rinsed if necessary

1–2 **garlic cloves**, crushed

1 tablespoon **Dijon mustard**

125 ml (4 fl oz) **olive oil**

1 teaspoon crumbled **thyme**

lemon juice, to taste

pepper

100 g ($3^1/2$ oz) **Danish blue cheese** or another **strong creamy blue cheese**

200 g (7 oz) **cream cheese**

50 ml (2 fl oz) **milk**

4 tablespoons chopped **chives**, plus extra for garnish

50 g (2 oz) **shelled walnuts**, chopped, plus extra for garnish

blue cheese and walnut dip

1 Put the Danish blue and the cream cheese into a bowl with the milk and whisk until smooth. Fold in the chives and walnuts. Transfer to a serving bowl and serve garnished with a few chopped walnuts and some chives.

Makes 400 ml (14 fl oz)

Preparation time: 10 minutes

FOOD FACT

Blue cheeses are curd cheeses which have bacteria injected into them so that they develop blue or green veining. Although the best blue cheeses are intensely individual, they share a sharp flavour and a crumbly texture, which makes them very useful in cooking.

250 g (8 oz) deli-marinated **artichoke hearts**

2 tablespoons **olive oil**

2 teaspoons **coarse grain mustard**

2 teaspoons **clear honey**

25 g (1 oz) **Parmesan cheese**, finely grated

150 ml (¹/₄ pint) **soured cream**

salt and **pepper**

creamy artichoke dip with mustard and parmesan

1 Put the artichoke hearts into a food processor or blender with the olive oil, mustard, honey and Parmesan and blend until you have a fairly smooth paste.

2 Transfer the dip to a serving bowl, season with salt and pepper and fold in the soured cream. Serve immediately.

Makes 400 ml (14 fl oz)

Preparation time: 10 minutes

TIP
Artichoke hearts are sold in cans and jars. They are excellent in salads and can be sautéed in butter and sprinkled with parsley or chervil and served as a vegetable dish or tossed with pasta and Parmesan cheese to make a quick supper.

50 g (2 oz) **basil leaves**

1 **garlic clove**, crushed

2 tablespoons **pine nuts**

$^1/_4$ teaspoon **sea salt**

6–8 tablespoons **extra virgin olive oil**

2 tablespoons grated **Parmesan cheese**

pepper

150 g (5 oz) **crème fraîche**

basil leaves, to serve

pesto and crème fraîche dip

1 First make the pesto. Put the basil, garlic, pine nuts and salt into a food processor and work to a smooth paste. Slowly add the oil until the texture is soft but not too runny, then add the Parmesan and pepper to taste, and mix. Transfer to a bowl and cover with clingfilm. Pesto can be kept for up to 3 days in the refrigerator.

2 To make the dip, put the crème fraîche into a bowl and lightly mix in 2 tablespoons of the pesto, so that the crème fraîche is streaked with the pesto. Serve scattered with basil leaves.

Makes 150 ml ($^1/_4$ pint)

Preparation time: 10 minutes

---

200 ml (7 fl oz) **natural yogurt**

7.5 cm (3 inch) piece of **cucumber**, peeled and coarsely grated or chopped

2 tablespoons **chopped mint**

pinch of **ground cumin**

squeeze of **lemon** or **lime juice**

pepper

mint sprigs, to garnish

cucumber and mint raita

A mild-flavoured and refreshing Indian yogurt dish, this is the perfect accompaniment to any spicy, highly seasoned meat, fish or vegetable. A little chopped fresh chilli or coriander leaves or some mint sauce can also be added.

1 Put the yogurt into a bowl and beat lightly with a fork or whisk until smooth. Add the cucumber, mint, cumin, lemon or lime juice and pepper and stir to combine. Cover and refrigerate until required. Serve chilled, garnished with mint sprigs.

Makes 300 ml ($^1/_2$ pint)

Preparation time: 10 minutes, plus chilling

herbed yogurt dip

1 Put the basil, parsley, lemon thyme, garlic, almonds, lemon rind and olive oil into a small food processor or blender and work to a fine paste. Season with salt and pepper.

2 Put the yogurt into a serving bowl and fold through the herb mixture, creating a marbled effect. Serve immediately.

Makes 350 ml (12 fl oz)

Preparation time: 10 minutes

TIP

Greek yogurt makes an excellent base for a quick dip. Mix chopped or grated cucumber, chopped mint and garlic with yogurt to make tzatziki; blend roasted and deseeded yellow peppers in a food processor with soy sauce, chopped coriander, yogurt and a little pepper for a piquant and vivid appetizer, or, if you're really pushed for time, simply stir in some curry powder or paste.

20 g (³/₄ oz) **basil** leaves

15 g (¹/₂ oz) **flat leaf parsley**

15 g (¹/₂ oz) **lemon thyme**

1 **garlic clove**, peeled

25 g (1 oz) **toasted almonds**

grated **rind of 1 lemon**

5 tablespoons **olive oil**

250 g (8 oz) **Greek yogurt**

salt and **pepper**

2 tablespoons **olive oil**

1 small **onion**, chopped

1 **garlic clove**, crushed

300 ml ($^1/_2$ pint) **crème fraîche**

25 g (1 oz) **dried onion soup mix**

3 tablespoons chopped **parsley**, plus a little extra for garnish

2 tablespoons **milk**

classic french onion dip

This dip is very good served with thin slices of French bread, sprinkled with a little Parmesan cheese and toasted.

1 Heat the olive oil in a frying pan. Add the onion and cook over a moderate heat for 5 minutes, then add the garlic and continue to cook for 2 minutes until just starting to colour. Remove from the heat and allow to cool.

2 Combine the onion mixture with the crème fraîche, onion soup mix, parsley and milk. Transfer to a serving dish and leave to stand in the refrigerator for 1 hour to set. Stir well and serve, garnished with parsley.

Makes 400 ml (14 fl oz)

Preparation time: 10 minutes, plus cooling and chilling

Cooking time: 7 minutes

crab dip with horseradish

1 Put the egg yolks, vinegar, mustard and horseradish into a food processor or blender, season with salt and pepper and blend until pale and creamy. With the motor running, gradually pour in all the oil. You should have a thick, glossy mixture.

2 Transfer the mayonnaise to a bowl, stir in the crab and spring onions and serve immediately.

Makes 300 ml (¹/₂ pint)

Preparation time: 15 minutes

2 **egg yolks**

2 teaspoons **red wine vinegar**

1 teaspoon **Dijon mustard**

1¹/₂ tablespoons **creamed horseradish**

150 ml (¹/₄ pint) **olive oil**

170 g (5 ³/₄ oz) can **white crab meat,** drained

3 **spring onions**, chopped

salt and **pepper**

indonesian peanut dipping sauce

This recipe was inspired by satay sauce, the rich, spicy, nutty Indonesian concoction made from peanuts, peanut butter, ginger and chilli. In this recipe the sauce is thicker and richer than usual, so that it can be used as a dip. It is delicious with any type of vegetable brochette or kebab, with chunky pieces of grilled vegetables and grilled skewered meats, particularly chicken.

1 Heat the oil in a saucepan and fry the onion, garlic, ginger and ground peanuts for 10 minutes to develop the flavours. Add the chilli powder, soy sauce, peanut butter, sugar, lime juice and coconut cream, stirring well to combine. Bring to the boil, then reduce the heat and cook gently for a further 10 minutes.

2 Transfer the sauce to a bowl and allow to cool, then cover and chill for at least 30 minutes.

Makes 250 ml (8 fl oz)

Preparation time: 10 minutes, plus cooling and chilling

Cooking time: 20–25 minutes

2 tablespoons **sunflower oil**

1 small **onion**, finely grated

2 **garlic cloves**, crushed

2.5 cm (1 inch) piece of **fresh root ginger**, peeled and grated

50 g (2 oz) **dry roasted peanuts**, ground in a blender or nut mill

large pinch of **hot chilli powder**

$^1/_2$ teaspoon **soy sauce**

2 tablespoons **crunchy peanut butter**

1–2 tablespoons **muscovado sugar**

2 tablespoons **lime juice**

200 ml (7 fl oz) carton **coconut cream**

15 medium **chillies**

250 g (8 oz) **granulated sugar**

150 ml (^{1}/$_4$ pint) **rice wine vinegar**

150 ml (^{1}/$_4$ pint) **water**

^{1}/$_2$ teaspoon **salt**

^{1}/$_4$ teaspoon **pepper**

juice of 1 **lemon**

sweet chilli sauce

This Thai sauce is particularly good with Thai fish cakes and deep-fried chicken or fish. It will keep for up to 1 month in the refrigerator.

1 Wearing a pair of plastic gloves, remove the seeds from the chillies and finely chop the flesh. Place the chillies in a saucepan with the sugar, rice vinegar and water. Heat gently to dissolve the sugar then increase the heat and simmer briskly for 20–25 minutes or until the liquid has reduced to a syrup.

2 Remove the pan from the heat and leave to cool. Add the salt, pepper and lemon juice. Pour the sauce into a container and store in the refrigerator until required.

Makes 300 ml (^{1}/$_2$ pint)

Preparation time: 15 minutes, plus cooling

Cooking time: 20–25 minutes

szechuan dipping sauce

A hot peppery dipping sauce, which takes its name from the fiery style of cooking of the Szechuan province of China. Although hot, it is also slightly sweet and spicy. Serve with Crudités (see page 63) or robust grilled vegetables. This sauce will keep for several weeks in the refrigerator without the spring onions and coriander.

1 In a screw-top jar, combine the soy sauce, sesame oil, lime juice, vinegar, chilli sauce, honey, garlic, sesame seeds and ginger. Shake well to mix. Chill in the refrigerator for a few hours so that the flavours can mingle and develop.

2 Just before serving, stir in the spring onions and coriander.

Makes 65 ml (2 1/2 fl oz)

Preparation time: 10 minutes, plus chilling

3 tablespoons **soy sauce**

2 tablespoons **light sesame oil**

2 tablespoons **lime juice**

1 tablespoon **rice wine vinegar**

1 tablespoon **sweet chilli sauce**

1 tablespoon **clear honey**

2 **garlic cloves**, finely chopped

1 teaspoon **toasted sesame seeds**

2.5 cm (1 inch) piece of **fresh root ginger**, peeled and finely grated

2 large **spring onions**, finely chopped

1 tablespoon finely **chopped coriander**

6 sheets **filo pastry**, 31 x 21 cm (12 1/2 x 8 1/2 inches), defrosted if frozen

75 g (3 oz) **butter**, melted

175 g (6 oz) **Emmenthal cheese**, finely grated

filo and emmenthal wafers

These crisp savoury wafers are composed of gossamer thin sheets of filo pastry layered with butter and finely grated Emmenthal cheese. They make excellent biscuits to serve with drinks and dips, and can be stored in an airtight container for 3–4 days.

1 Lightly brush 1 sheet of filo pastry with butter and scatter with a little of the cheese. Put a second sheet on top, brush with melted butter and scatter with more cheese. Repeat with a third sheet, finishing with the cheese. Do the same with the remaining 3 sheets of filo pastry so that you have 2 stacks of pastry. Using a 7.5 cm (3 inch) plain round pastry cutter, cut the filo layers into circles and place them on a heavy baking sheet. Alternatively, cut the pastry into rectangular 10 x 3 cm (4 x 1 1/4 inch) wafers.

2 Bake the wafers in a preheated oven at 180°C (350°F), Gas Mark 4 for 15 minutes until crisp and light brown. Remove from the baking sheet and cool on a wire rack.

Makes 22 round biscuits or 42 rectangular ones

Preparation time: 10 minutes

Cooking time: 15 minutes

125 g (4 oz) **plain flour**

75 g (3 oz) **unsalted butter**, cut into small pieces

1 tablespoon **English mustard powder**

pinch of **cayenne pepper**

pinch of **salt**

125 g (4 oz) **mature Cheddar cheese**, finely grated

40–50 g (1$^{1}/_{2}$–2 oz) **Parmesan cheese**, finely grated

2 tablespoons **black mustard seeds**

1 tablespoon **poppy seeds**

seeded cheese sablés

Serve these crisp savoury biscuits with dips, soup, raw vegetable salads like Crudités (see page 63), and roasted or grilled vegetables. They are perfect with cheese and chutney too, and also good as a cocktail biscuit. They can be cut into any shape, served hot or cold, and they will freeze well.

1 Work the flour, butter, mustard, cayenne and salt in a food processor until the mixture resembles fine breadcrumbs. Add the Cheddar and continue to process for a few seconds until the mixture begins to come together to make a soft dough. Turn on to a lightly floured surface and knead gently. Wrap in clingfilm and refrigerate for about 30 minutes.

2 Roll out the pastry on a lightly floured surface to about 2.5 mm ($^{1}/_{8}$ inch) thick. Cut into circles with a 6 cm (2$^{1}/_{2}$ inch) fluted pastry cutter. Knead the trimmings together, roll out and cut out more circles.

3 Line 2 heavy baking sheets with nonstick baking paper and place the sablés on them. Sprinkle with Parmesan and dust with mustard and poppy seeds. Bake in a preheated oven at 200°C (400°F), Gas Mark 6 for 9–12 minutes until crisp and light golden. Transfer to a wire rack with a palette knife. Serve hot, or set aside to cool and store in an airtight container to serve later.

Makes about 30

Preparation time: 20 minutes, plus chilling

Cooking time: 9–12 minutes

cheesy crisps

These can be served as a savoury bite with drinks, or as an accompaniment with salsas and dips of your choice. The cheese can be mixed with 25 g (1 oz) chopped walnuts, pecans or hazelnuts, and seasoned with fresh thyme, ground black pepper, a little paprika or cayenne pepper. When cold, the crisps can be stored in an airtight container for about 1 week or frozen for several weeks. If they soften, return them to a hot oven to crisp up.

1 Line several baking sheets with nonstick baking paper. Place 2 mounds of cheese on each sheet, no more than 8 cm ($3^1/_2$ inches) in diameter and at least 10 cm (4 inches) apart. As it cooks the cheese will spread and form rough biscuit shapes.

2 Bake the crisps in a preheated oven at 220°C (425°F), Gas Mark 7 for 10 minutes until the cheese bubbles and begins to turn a very pale cream colour. Too golden in colour and it will taste bitter.

3 Allow the crisps to cool slightly, then transfer them with a spatula to a wire rack to cool completely. Serve or store as required.

Makes 8–10

Preparation time: 10 minutes

Cooking time: 10 minutes per batch

125 g (4 oz) **mature farmhouse** or **vegetarian Cheddar, Gruyère** or **raclette cheese**, coarsely grated or diced

4 small **flour tortillas**

1 tablespoon **olive oil**

tortilla chips

1 Cut each tortilla into 8 triangles, place on a baking sheet and brush with a little oil. Bake in a preheated oven at 200°C (400°F), Gas Mark 6 for 10–12 minutes until golden and crisp. Allow to cool.

Makes 32

Preparation time: 5 minutes

Cooking time: 10–12 minutes

TIP

As a change from plain tortilla chips, and to add both flavour and colour, mix a little paprika and salt with the olive oil when you moisten the tortillas before putting them in the oven.

Starter dough

250 ml (8 fl oz) **warm water**

$^1/_4$ teaspoon **dry active yeast**

375 g (12 oz) **strong white flour**

$^1/_2$ teaspoon **sugar**

Bread dough

$1^1/_2$ teaspoons **dry active yeast**

900 ml ($1^1/_2$ pints) **warm water**

1 teaspoon **sugar**

750 g ($1^1/_2$ lb) **strong white flour**

250 g (8 oz) **semolina**, plus extra for sprinkling

$1^1/_2$ tablespoons **salt**

sourdough bread

1 Four days before making the bread, prepare the starter dough. Pour the warm water into a small bowl and stir in the yeast to dissolve it. Add about 4 tablespoons of the flour and the sugar and leave to froth in a warm place for 10 minutes. Work the mixture into the remaining flour, cover with clingfilm and leave in a warm place for at least 3 days.

2 To begin the bread dough, dissolve the yeast in 150 ml ($^1/_4$ pint) of the warm water, add the sugar and 4 tablespoons of the flour and leave to froth for 10 minutes. Transfer to a large bowl and gradually work in 125 g (4 oz) of the starter dough (refrigerate the rest and use as required), the remaining warm water and flour, the semolina and salt until a sticky, slightly lumpy dough forms.

3 Transfer the dough to an oiled bowl, cover with oiled clingfilm and leave in a warm place for several hours to double in size.

4 Carefully tip out the dough on to a floured surface, cut off about 125 g (4 oz) and add it to the starter dough mixture. Cut the remaining dough in half and shape each piece into a flat round. Roll the dough up, turn it 180° and repeat the rolling. Transfer to a well-floured baking sheet, sprinkle the surface with semolina and cover with a clean tea towel.

5 Leave the dough to rise for 1–2 hours, until doubled in size. Score the surface with a sharp knife and bake in a preheated oven at 230°C (450°F), Gas Mark 8 for 30 minutes. Cool on a wire rack.

Makes 2 round loaves

Preparation time: 40 minutes, plus standing and rising

Cooking time: 30 minutes

6 white **pitta breads**

3 **garlic cloves**, crushed

1 tablespoon **dried mixed herbs**

6 tablespoons **olive oil**

2 teaspoons **mild chilli powder**

2 teaspoons **paprika**

pitta chips

1 Split open the pittas then cut each half into quarters. Divide them equally between 2 large roasting tins. In the first tin rub the garlic, mixed herbs and half the olive oil into the bread. Rub the chilli powder, paprika and the remaining oil into the second batch of bread.

2 Bake in a preheated oven at 200°C (400°F), Gas Mark 6 for 15 minutes or until lightly golden in colour and crispy. Serve warm or cold with a selection of dips.

Makes 48

Preparation time: 10 minutes

Cooking time: 15 minutes

griddle bread

1 Sift the flours and salt into the bowl of a food mixer. Stir in the yeast and then, with the dough hook turning, gradually add the water and oil to form a soft dough. Knead for 8–10 minutes, until smooth and elastic.

2 Transfer the dough to an oiled bowl, cover with a tea towel and leave to rise in a warm place for 1 hour, until doubled in size.

3 Divide the dough into eight pieces and roll out each one on a lightly floured surface to form an oval (about the same size as commercial pitta breads), brush with a little oil and leave to rise for about 10 minutes.

4 Heat a griddle or heavy-based pan until really hot and cook the breads for about 2 minutes on each side, until spotted with brown and puffed up. Serve immediately.

Makes 8

Preparation time: 15 minutes, plus rising

Cooking time: 4 minutes per batch

500 g (1 lb) **plain flour**

250 g (8 oz) **wholemeal flour**

2 teaspoons **salt**

1 teaspoon **fast-acting yeast**

450 ml ($^3/_4$ pint) **warm water**

1 tablespoon **extra virgin olive oil**, plus extra for brushing

4 large **baking potatoes**

4–6 tablespoons **olive oil**

$^1/_2$ teaspoon **salt**

1–2 teaspoons **chilli powder**,
to taste

chilli potato wedges

**Use as little or as much chilli powder as you like, to coat these
oven-roasted potato wedges.**

1 Cut each potato into 8 wedges
and place in a large bowl. Add the
oil, salt and chilli powder and toss
until evenly coated.

2 Transfer the potatoes to a
baking sheet and roast in a
preheated oven at 220°C (425°F),
Gas Mark 7 for 15 minutes. Turn
them over and cook for a further
15 minutes. Turn once more and
cook for a final 25–30 minutes
until crisp and golden.

3 Allow to cool slightly and serve
with a spicy dip.

Makes 32

Preparation time: 5 minutes

Cooking time: about 1 hour

chicken skewers with fruit and nut couscous

1 Cut the chicken into long thin strips, place them in a shallow dish and add the olive oil, garlic, spices and lemon juice.
Stir well then cover and leave to marinate for 2 hours. Thread the chicken strips on to 8 small, presoaked wooden skewers.

2 Griddle or grill the chicken skewers for 4–5 minutes on each side, until charred and cooked through. Serve with the fruit and nut couscous, garnished with pomegranate seeds, lemon wedges and coriander sprigs, and a selection of dips.

Serves 4

Preparation time: 20–30 minutes, plus marinating

Cooking time: 8–10 minutes, plus couscous

FRUIT AND NUT COUSCOUS

Pour 600 ml (1 pint) stock over 175 g (6 oz) couscous and steam for 8–10 minutes. Meanwhile, fry 1 small onion, 1 crushed garlic clove and 1 teaspoon each ground cinnamon, cumin, pepper and ginger in 2 tablespoons olive oil. Mix in 125 g (4 oz) chopped dried fruit and 50 g (2 oz) chopped, toasted blanched almonds and remove from the heat. Stir the fruit and nut mixture into the couscous with 2 tablespoons oil, 1 tablespoon lemon juice and 2 tablespoons chopped coriander and season to taste.

500 g (1 lb) skinless **chicken breast fillets**

2 tablespoons **extra virgin olive oil**

2 **garlic cloves**, crushed

$^{1}/_{2}$ teaspoon each **ground cumin, turmeric** and **paprika**

2 teaspoons **lemon juice**

dips, to serve

To garnish
seeds from $^{1}/_{2}$ **pomegranate**

lemon wedges

coriander sprigs

500 g (1 lb) **beef rump steak,** cut lengthways into thin strips

Marinade
100 ml (3 ¹/₂ fl oz) **coconut milk**

2 tablespoons **soy sauce**

1 **red chilli,** finely chopped

2 **garlic cloves,** crushed

grated rind and juice of 1 **lime**

To serve
crisp **green salad leaves**

Indonesian Peanut Dipping Sauce (see page 45)

lime wedges

beef satay

1 Put all the marinade ingredients into a bowl and mix together. Add the beef slices and mix well. Cover and leave to marinate in the refrigerator for at least 4 hours. Soak 8 bamboo skewers in water for at least 30 minutes.

2 Drain the beef, keeping the marinade to one side, then thread the beef in a zig-zag pattern on to the prepared skewers. Put the skewers into a lightly oiled grill pan and cook under a preheated grill for 7–8 minutes, turning them and spooning over a little of the marinade from time to time while they are cooking. Serve the beef strips on crisp green salad leaves with some peanut sauce and garnish with lime wedges.

Serves 4

Preparation time: 15 minutes

Cooking time: 7–8 minutes

750 g (1¹/₂ lb) **assorted vegetables**, such as peppers, courgettes, aubergines, baby sweetcorn, onions, French beans, cauliflower, mushrooms, chopped

sunflower oil, for frying

fresh herbs or **salad leaves**, to garnish

Aïoli (see page 34), to serve

Batter
1 large **egg**

200 ml (7 fl oz) **lager**, very well chilled

125 g (4 oz) **plain flour**

¹/₂ teaspoon **baking powder**

salt and **pepper**

vegetable tempura

1 About 20 minutes before cooking, prepare the batter. With a small wire whisk, beat the egg well in a large bowl, Still beating, add the lager in a thin stream. Sift the flour, baking powder and a pinch of salt into another bowl, stir in pepper to taste and tip on top of the egg and lager. Stir with the whisk, barely enough to mix. Don't overbeat. Cover and leave to stand for about 10 minutes.

2 Heat the oil in a deep-fryer to 190°C (375°F). Dip the vegetables in the batter, one type at a time. Fry no more than 6 pieces at once or the temperature of the oil will drop and make the batter greasy. Courgettes, onions, cauliflower, baby sweetcorn and mushrooms take 3–5 minutes; peppers, aubergines and beans about 3 minutes. The batter should be puffy, crisp and golden, the vegetables just tender.

3 Transfer the vegetables to an ovenproof dish or tray lined with kitchen paper and keep warm in a preheated oven at 190°C (375°F), Gas Mark 5 until they are all cooked. They will hold quite successfully for about 30 minutes.

4 Arrange the fritters on a large platter around a bowl of sauce, or pile about 9 fritters in the centre of individual plates and put a few spoonfuls of aïoli on the side. Garnish with herbs or salad leaves and serve immediately.

Serves 6–8

Preparation time: about 20 minutes, plus standing

Cooking time: 3–5 minutes per batch

crudités

This is the general term for a collection of crunchy raw vegetables and salad leaves eaten with the fingers and served with dips. Hummus (see page 34) is good with crudités, so too is Guacamole (see page 28) and Tapenade (see page 35). Crudités are the perfect start to any meal because they are light and refreshing and can be eaten informally with drinks or at the dining table. They also make a healthy lunch or snack with crusty bread as well as excellent party or finger food.

1 Choose firm, crisp vegetables, such as carrots, celery, cucumber, fennel, chicory, peppers, spring onions and lettuce hearts. These can be cut into finger-length pieces or sticks. Tight-headed vegetables, such as broccoli or cauliflower, can be broken into florets and small whole vegetables like cherry tomatoes, mushrooms, mange-touts, green beans and radishes can be left just as they are.

2 Wash and dry the vegetables well, then arrange them on a serving platter or individual plates.

3 Serve the dips and salsas of your choice separately.

Preparation time: 5–10 minutes per portion

Allow 125–150 g (4–5 oz) **assorted vegetables** per person with a selection of 3–4 dips, salsas and sauces

index

acknowledgements

Executive Editor: Sarah Ford
Editor: Rachel Lawrence
Executive Art Editor: Geoff Fennell
Designer: Briony Chappell
Production Controller: Louise Hall
Index: Indexing Specialists

Photography: Gus Filgate
Food styling and additional recipes:
David Morgan